Ultimate FACTIVITY Collection

W9-ATT-904

Discover LEGO® *Star Wars*™ with fun, fascinating activities that help you learn as you play. All the activities can be done right on the page—you just need a few colored pencils and some imagination!

Contents

This book belongs to:

Noah Smith

CHAPTER 1 ◉ The Force is Strong

Anakin Skywalker

Anakin is trained to use the light side of the Force as a Jedi, but Palpatine persuades him to join the dark side.

Yoda

Yoda is a Jedi Grand Master and a member of the Jedi High Council. He is the oldest and wisest Jedi, and is very powerful.

Obi-Wan Kenobi

Obi-Wan Kenobi is a skillful Jedi who trains Anakin, and then years later, Luke Skywalker.

The galaxy is divided between good and evil. The two sides are wrestling for control and are aided by a mysterious Force. Not everyone is who they seem!

© 2016 LEGO

© 2016 LEGO

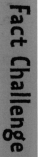

Emperor Palpatine

As Emperor, Palpatine is head of the government. He has a secret identity—he is really a Sith Lord in disguise.

Duels

Sith and Jedi often battle in lightsaber duels. Using a lightsaber requires great Force power as lightsabers are dangerous weapons.

Darth Vader

Anakin Skywalker has turned to the dark side of the Force. He now fights for the Sith rather than the Jedi.

Jedi Luke

Luke Skywalker becomes a Jedi Knight after training with Yoda. He fights against the evil Empire.

© 2016 LEGO

© 2016 LEGO

Force Rules

Complete the Force facts

The Force is a mysterious and powerful energy that flows through all living things. It can only be used by "Force-sensitive" beings. Jedi use the light side of the Force for good. Sith are drawn to the dark side, believing it will give them greater power.

Use the Force!

Read about the Force and then fill in the Force facts.

Jedi and the Force

Knowledge of the Force gives the Jedi great power. They use the light side of the Force to try to maintain peace and justice throughout the galaxy. The Force can be used in many different, and powerful, ways.

Creature communication

On Utapau, Obi-Wan Kenobi chooses to ride Boga, a varactyl. He communicates with her by using the Force, and is able to sense her moods.

Physical strength

On Dagobah, Yoda trains Luke in the ways of the Jedi. He teaches him to have control—by doing headstands and moving objects with the Force!

Force ghost

After death, it is possible for a Jedi to become one with the Force and appear as a Force ghost. Yoda and Obi-Wan Kenobi appear as Force ghosts to Luke.

Mind tricks

Powerful Jedi can use the Force to confuse their enemies with mind tricks. But some people, such as villain Jabba the Hutt, can block these mind tricks!

Grand Master Yoda

Yoda is a Grand Master of the Force. During his long life, Yoda helps to train many great Jedi in the ways of the Force, including Obi-Wan Kenobi and Luke Skywalker.

THE FORCE

1 The power of the Force can only be used by those who are ✎ _____

2 Jedi use the ✎ _____ side of the Force to battle evil.

3 To master the Force, Luke goes to Dagobah to ✎ _____ with Yoda.

4 Obi-Wan Kenobi becomes one with the Force, appearing to Luke as a ✎ _____

5 Jedi can use ✎ _____ to try and fool their enemies.

6 Yoda is a ✎ _____ of the Force, training many Jedi.

Jedi Training
Complete the Jedi checklist

A Jedi must go through years of training before becoming a full Jedi Knight. A Padawan is a young Jedi apprentice who is taught by a wise Jedi Knight or Master.

Time to train, young Padawan!

Read about Jedi training. Then find the stickers and tick off the Jedi training goals.

Jedi training academies

Force-sensitive young children are enrolled in a training academy. They are taught many things, including the ways of the Force, before they can graduate and be chosen by a Knight or Master for further training.

The Council advises all Jedi.

Padawans must pass many tests.

The life of a Jedi is not easy.

Jedi High Council

The Jedi High Council is made up of twelve wise and powerful Jedi Masters. They guide the Jedi Order and have a say in all Padawans' training and trials.

Jedi Checklist

1 Selection

Padawans are selected by Masters for training. They will be taught how to control their power, emotions, and the Force.

Prepare to duel!

2 Combat

Tough one-to-one training with their Masters teaches young Padawans the skills of lightsaber combat.

3 Field trips

Padawans are sent with their Master on missions and are expected to battle alongside them for experience.

4 Knighthood

Once their Master feels they are ready, a Padawan can take the Jedi Trials to become a full Jedi Knight.

5 Teaching

New Jedi Knights can take on a Padawan of their own to train in the ways of the Jedi.

Find the **stickers** at the back of the book.

Use the Force
Match the story parts

The Jedi often find themselves in tricky situations during their missions. They use their wits, skill, and the Force to overcome problems on their quests.

Read the descriptions and draw a line to link each problem with its solution. Then add the stickers.

Force Energy

Only **Force-sensitive** beings, such as this Ithorian Jedi Master, can use the Force. It takes many **years** and **patience** to master it.

I feel the Force!

Problems

Stormtrooper trouble
Obi-Wan Kenobi and Luke Skywalker have been stopped by stormtroopers and they need to get off Tatooine fast!

Wampa attack
On Hoth, Luke wakes to find his feet frozen to the ceiling of a wampa cave. A hungry wampa is waiting nearby!

Stuck Starfighter
After a bumpy landing, Luke's X-wing starfighter is stuck in a swamp on Dagobah.

Cloud City duel
After a duel with Darth Vader, who is trying to make Luke join the dark side, Luke is left clinging for his life.

Solutions

Force strength

After Luke tries but fails, Yoda uses the Force to lift Luke's X-wing free from the swamp.

Force movement

Summoning his lightsaber by using the Force, Luke cuts himself free from the wampa cave with it and escapes.

Force call

Luke uses the Force to communicate with Leia, who comes with his friends on the *Millennium Falcon* to rescue him.

Mind tricks

Using Force mind tricks, Obi-Wan persuades the Empire's stormtroopers to let them pass.

Find the **answers** on page 97.

Find the **stickers** at the back of the book.

Lift Off

Complete the spacecraft

Battles are often fought in the air. There are many different starships in the galaxy, each equipped with special features that help their pilots to out-fly their enemies.

Read about the starships and then choose the correct stickers to fill the gaps.

Gunship

These gunships are used for **moving troops**. Two **huge engines** allow them to speed across the galaxy.

Imperial crew

The Imperial pilot works for the Empire and is ready for action with his blaster rifle.

Star Destroyer

The Empire's mighty starship, an Imperial Star Destroyer, has **awesome firepower** and a sleek, streamlined shape.

Find the **stickers** at the back of the book.

Millennium Falcon

One of the fastest ships in the galaxy, the *Millennium Falcon* uses a **hyperdrive** to speed past enemy Imperial fighters.

© 2016 LEGO

TIE Interceptor

Propelled by **twin ion engines**, TIE Interceptors are fast and have four **laser cannons**.

ARC-170 Starfighter

A starfighter and **heavy bomber**, the ARC-170 is used to escort smaller fighters. These powerful spacecraft are flown by **clone pilots**.

© 2016 LEGO

●·········· **Enemy fire**

Wing-mounted laser cannons protect the ARC-170 Starfighter.

11

Pick a Padawan

Match the Padawan to their Master

When traveling on missions with their Master, a Padawan learns how to be a Jedi. They must work together—with a Padawan learning from the wisdom and experience of their Master.

A Padawan is a Jedi apprentice!

Read the decriptions opposite, add the stickers then write the Padawan's name.

Yoda

*In exile on Dagobah, **wise Master Yoda** trains someone with great potential and a familiar name.*

This apprentice has **Force powers** in the **family**.

My name is:
Luke

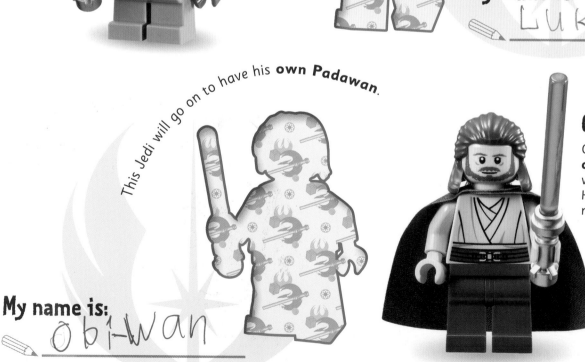

This Jedi will go on to have his **own Padawan**.

Qui-Gon Jinn

*Qui-Gon was **defeated** in a duel with a Sith apprentice. His Padawan could do nothing to stop it.*

My name is:
obi-wan

Padawans

Anakin Skywalker

After the **death of Qui-Gon**, his Padawan agrees to take Anakin as his own apprentice.

Luke Skywalker

Luke recieves training from an extremely wise, old **Jedi Grand Master**.

Ahsoka Tano

Yoda assigned talented Ahsoka to a **Jedi Knight** to teach him responsibility.

Obi-Wan Kenobi

Obi-Wan is Padawan to a Jedi Master **beaten in battle** with a Sith.

Obi-Wan Kenobi

Obi-Wan Kenobi was once a Padawan, too. But when his **Master Qui-Gon** is beaten in battle, Obi-Wan agrees to take on his own Padawan.

This Jedi will turn to the **dark side**.

My name is:
Anakin

This young Padawan has **great potential**.

My name is:
Ahsoka tano

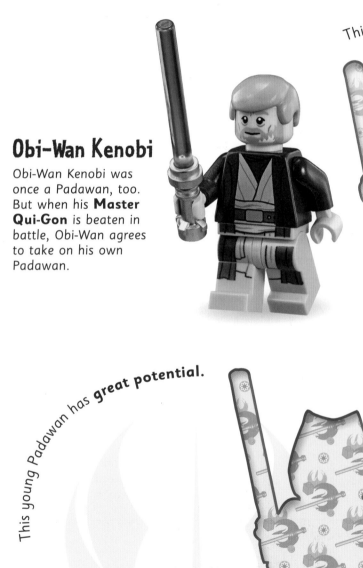

Anakin Skywalker

As a hot-headed Jedi Knight, Anakin was **assigned a talented young Padawan** by Master Yoda.

Jedi vs. Sith

Complete the lightsaber duels

Jedi and Sith are sworn enemies and must often face each other in dangerous lightsaber duels. Here, Darth Maul, a Sith apprentice, is battling two Jedi, Qui-Gon Jinn and Obi-Wan Kenobi.

Read the story, then write and draw the ending in the final box.

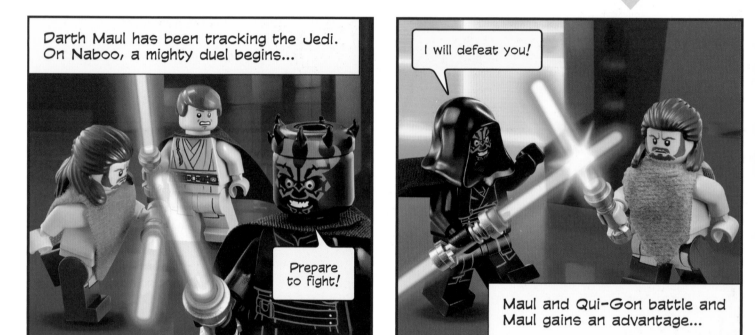

Darth Maul has been tracking the Jedi. On Naboo, a mighty duel begins...

Prepare to fight!

I will defeat you!

Maul and Qui-Gon battle and Maul gains an advantage...

Evreyone

Dies

THE END!

In another duel, Luke Skywalker is taking on two powerful Sith Lords by himself. Will he be overpowered?

Read the story, then write and draw the ending in the final box.

Qui-Gon Jinn

Qui-Gon is a **skillful Jedi Master** who fights to protect the galaxy from evil forces. His **lightsaber skills** have saved him from trouble and won him many duels.

Give in to the dark side!

Never!

Luke battles fiercely with Darth Vader, defeating him.

I won't do it!

Luke refuses to destroy Vader as it would mean turning to the dark side.

You will suffer!

Furious, Palpatine unleashes his Force lightning on Luke.

Obi-Wan Kenobi

Training with Qui-Gon Jinn made Obi-Wan a powerful Jedi Master. He uses the **light side of the Force** to battle the Sith.

Evre one Dies

Luke Skywalker

Darth Vader tells Luke that he is **Luke's father**. Luke is determined to **fight against the dark side**, and he refuses to fight his own father.

THE END!

How will the stories **end**? You **decide!**

Force Challenge
Test your knowledge of Chapter 1

Answer each question. If you need help, look back through the chapter.

Now that you have finished the first chapter of the book, take the Force Challenge to show off your knowledge of the Force!

1. Find the sticker that best matches the description:

A starfighter lifted by Yoda from the swamps of Dagobah.

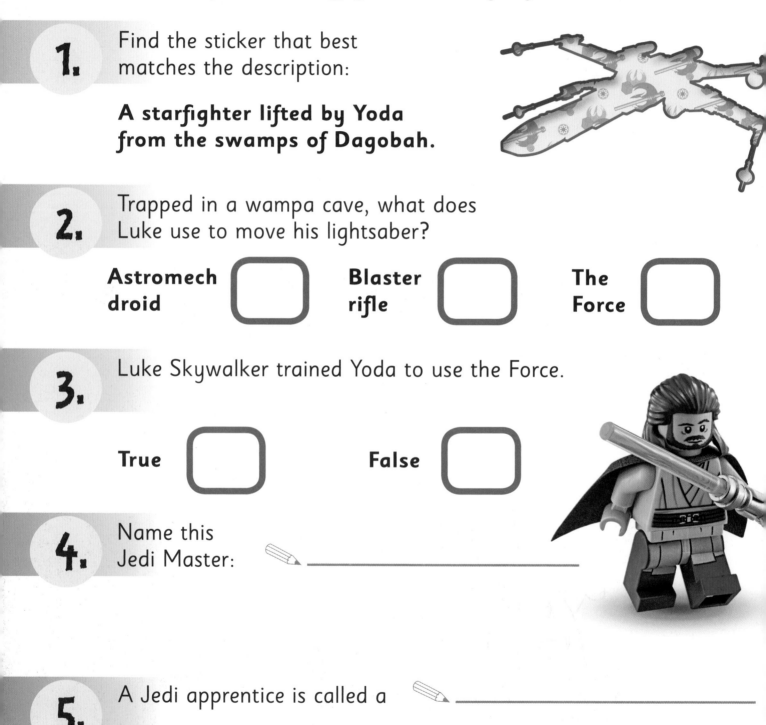

2. Trapped in a wampa cave, what does Luke use to move his lightsaber?

Astromech droid ☐   **Blaster rifle** ☐   **The Force** ☐

3. Luke Skywalker trained Yoda to use the Force.

True ☐   **False** ☐

4. Name this Jedi Master: _____

5. A Jedi apprentice is called a _____

Find the **answers** on page 97.

Well done—you have finished the Force Challenge! Fill this scene with your extra stickers.

CHAPTER 2 A Galaxy Far, Far Away

Gungans

Gungans are an amphibious species. They live in underwater bubble cities under Naboo's swamps.

The galaxy has many planets and moons that are home to lots of weird and wonderful creatures. All the species have their own skills, personalities, and allegiances.

Wookiees

Wookiees are native to the planet Kashyyyk. They are short-tempered and handy with a spear. Stay away from an angry Wookiee!

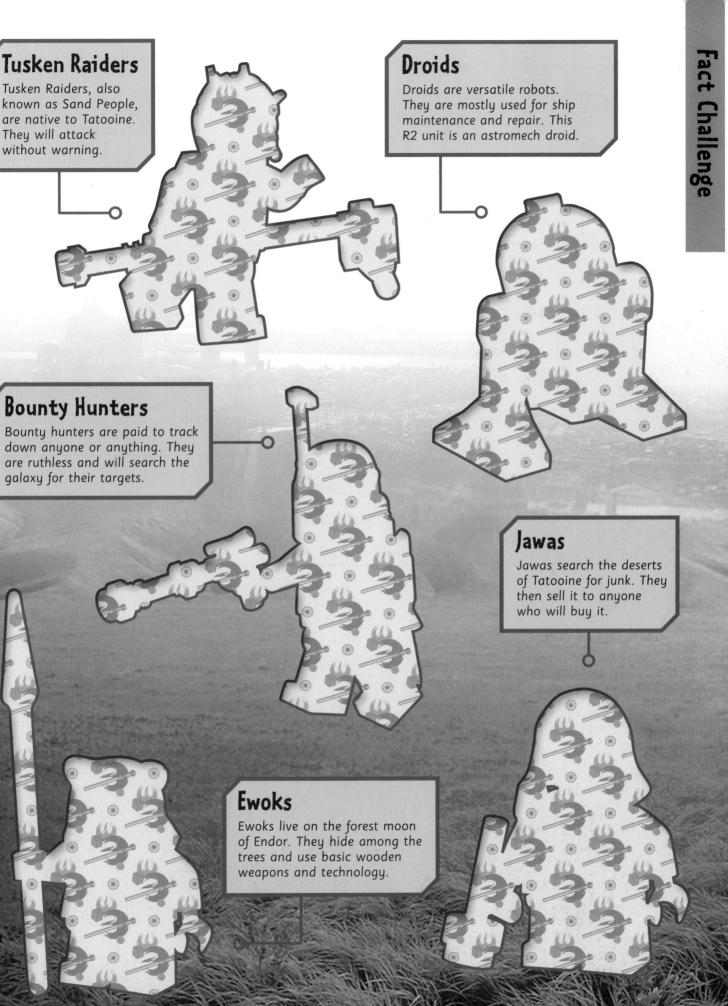

Tusken Raiders

Tusken Raiders, also known as Sand People, are native to Tatooine. They will attack without warning.

Droids

Droids are versatile robots. They are mostly used for ship maintenance and repair. This R2 unit is an astromech droid.

Bounty Hunters

Bounty hunters are paid to track down anyone or anything. They are ruthless and will search the galaxy for their targets.

Jawas

Jawas search the deserts of Tatooine for junk. They then sell it to anyone who will buy it.

Ewoks

Ewoks live on the forest moon of Endor. They hide among the trees and use basic wooden weapons and technology.

Planet Postcards

Design a postcard from Hoth

Every planet and moon in the galaxy has its own landscape, weather, and sights. No two planets are exactly the same.

Look at the postcards, then design and write a postcard from Hoth.

The Garden Planet Naboo

Naboo

Naboo is home to humans and Gungans. Its river cities are beautiful and it is the home of Padmé Amidala.

Naboo has green hills and swamps.

The Jedi Temple is on Coruscant.

CORUSCANT

Coruscant

Coruscant is a giant city planet. It is the heart of the galaxy and home of the government for the Galactic Republic and the Empire.

Hoth

Hoth is a freezing cold ice planet with only a small area that is habitable. The rebels set up Echo Base on Hoth to hide from the Imperial armies.

Hoth is covered in ice and snow.

Draw a picture for the front of your postcard.

Greetings from **HOTH**

Write a message on the back of your postcard.

Dear

Wampa

Wampas are furry creatures that live on Hoth. They have **razor-sharp claws** and **fangs**. Their white fur acts as **camouflage** in the snow. While on Hoth, a wampa managed to capture Luke Skywalker.

Tauntaun

Tauntauns have **adapted** for Hoth's freezing condtions. The rebels **ride the tauntauns** around the icy plains as they are more reliable in the cold than the rebels' vehicles.

Rebel trooper

On Hoth, rebel troopers wear insulated, **thermal uniforms**, **helmets**, and **snow goggles**. They must learn to battle the cold weather as well as the Empire.

21

Jawa Jumble
Put the droids back together

Jawas are always searching for scrap in the desert. They have already started to take apart these droids to rebuild and sell to people on Tatooine.

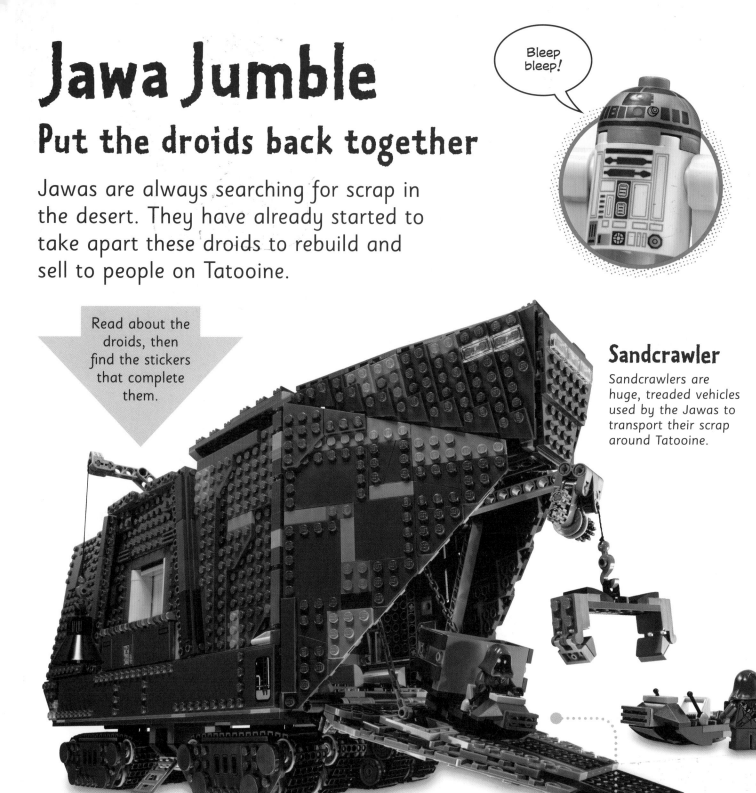

Bleep bleep!

Read about the droids, then find the stickers that complete them.

Sandcrawler

Sandcrawlers are huge, treaded vehicles used by the Jawas to transport their scrap around Tatooine.

Jawas

Small, hooded scavengers, Jawas use scrap parts to mend broken equipment and droids.

A giant ramp in the sandcrawler opens so that the Jawas can load and unload junk or bring out droids to sell.

R1-series droid

The R1-G4 is a starship technician that was abandoned by its owner. The Jawas found it in the desert.

Treadwell droid

This droid is made for repairs. Its many arms perform maintenance tasks.

C-3PO

This protocol droid is very intelligent. C-3PO is fluent in over six-million forms of communication!

Astromech

These small droids are used for repair work. They come with many tools stored in their compartments.

Gonk droid

GNK, or Gonk, droids are used as walking power generators.

R5-D4

R5-D4 is sold to Luke Skywalker's Uncle Lars on Tatooine. However, his head blew off so the Jawas sold him R2-D2 instead!

Find the **stickers** at the back of the book.

Tatooine Sandstorm

Draw the lost creatures and objects

Get me out of this dusty place!

Read about Tatooine. Draw and color the parts hidden by the sandstorm.

The planet of Tatooine is a dry desert with very little water. It is a dusty place where sandstorms are common. It is ruled by gangsters and is a base for smugglers, criminals, and other rogues.

Luke's Landspeeder

Obi-Wan Kenobi is hiding on Tatooine. He, Luke, R2-D2, and C-3PO take Luke's landspeeder to the town of Mos Eisley.

Tusken Raiders

These "**sand people**" are camouflaged for Tatooine's sandy landscape. They do not like strangers and wield clubs called **gaderffii**.

Greedo

Rodian **bounty hunter** Greedo is a dangerous enemy to have. He is determined to find and capture Han Solo.

Dewbacks

Dewbacks are popular **working monsters**. Sandtroopers ride these creatures on Tatooine as their speeder bikes are easily damaged by sand.

The desert planet can be a **dangerous** place.

Sandstorms make it difficult to see clearly.

Try to match the **colors** with the pictures opposite.

Monster Mayhem

Complete the monster scanner

There are all kinds of creatures to be found across the galaxy. Some are big and scary, but some are not as monstrous as they first appear. Recently, there have been sightings of a new monster...

Read about the new monster, then draw it and fill in the blanks.

> I think I would beat this new monster in a fight. It has bigger horns on its head than me, but four short legs.

> Unlike me, this new monster is not friendly. It has sharp teeth and looks hungry. Yikes!

Tauntaun

At first sniff, a tauntaun is fairly repulsive. But their smell is the worst thing about them. Tauntauns make reliable mounts and travel well across the snowdrifts of Hoth.

> I spotted a long tail covered with scales on this new monster. Rawr!

Wampa

That tauntaun had best watch out, or this furry wampa will gobble him right up. Wampas look cuddly, but they can be very vicious. Tauntauns—and Jedi—are their favorite foods.

Rancor

This rancor has captured Luke Skywalker! Being locked in Jabba the Hutt's dungeon has made it angry. And when it is angry, it opens its mouth to reveal terrifying rows of teeth!

Draw the monster based on the descriptions.

MONSTER SCANNER

This is a galactic warning of the highest level! A new monster has been spotted! It has _loo_ teeth and _horns_ on its head. It walks on _6b_ legs and has a long, scaly _spike_. The creature is thought to be carnivorous, so citizens should stay well away from it.

CURRENT REWARD: 10,000 credits

Endor's Ewoks
Draw a new Ewok friend!

Ewoks might look cute and cuddly living in their forest villages, but they are brave fighters. They will defend themselves and their allies with homemade weapons.

Don't mess with an Ewok!

Read about the Ewoks and then draw a new member of their tribe.

Chief Chirpa

Chief Chirpa leads the Ewok tribe. He agrees to help the rebels fight the Empire and welcomes Luke and his friends into the tribe.

Wicket

A friendly young Ewok, Wicket meets Princess Leia in the forest and rescues her from a stormtrooper.

Logray

When Logray first meets the rebels, he orders that Luke, Han and their friend, Chewbacca, are tied up! C-3PO persuades him to release them all.

Catapult

Sticks and spears

Bow and arrow

Ewok weapons

Ewoks use a lot of different weapons, including catapults, knives, spears, slingshots, bows, and arrows. During the Battle of Endor, they even throw large rocks at stormtroopers!

What **color** will your Ewok's **hood** be?

You could add a **pattern** to the hood.

What **color fur** will they have?

Draw a **weapon** for your Ewok.

This Ewok is named:

Bounty Hunters

Spot the galactic criminals

There are some real rogues lurking in the galaxy, ready to track down anyone or anything... if the price is right. These shady characters are known as "bounty hunters."

Read about the bounty hunters, then use the clues to identify them.

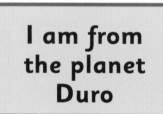

I don't hate Jedi

I am wearing a hat

I am from the planet Duro

Boba Fett

This bounty hunter is on a job from Darth Vader himself! Boba Fett pilots his own ship, *Slave I*, and is on a mission to locate Han Solo.

Bossk

Reptilian Bossk will hunt anyone, even tough Wookiees! He usually does jobs for the gangster Jabba the Hutt, but is also employed by Darth Vader.

Dengar

This bounty hunter is extra dangerous as he is part-cyborg. He has worked alongside other rogues, such as Boba Fett, but prefers to work on his own.

Cad Bane

Blue-skinned Cad Bane comes from the planet Duro. He has a grudging respect for Jedi, but will still hunt them down if paid to do so.

1 My name is:

_____

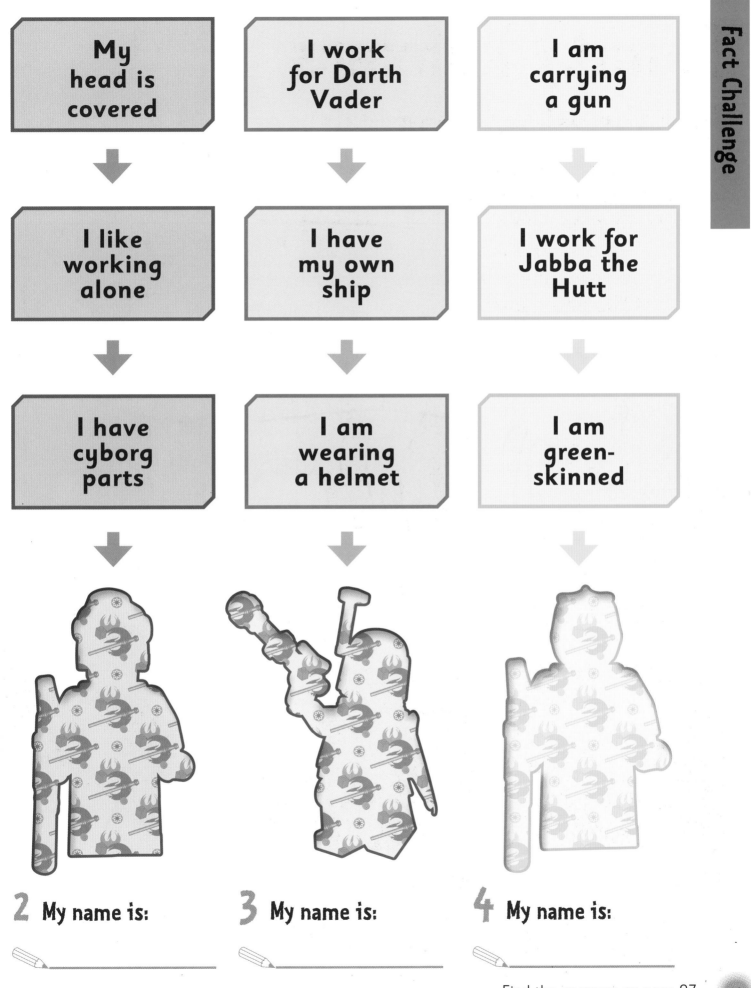

My head is covered

↓

I like working alone

↓

I have cyborg parts

↓

My work for Darth Vader

↓

I have my own ship

↓

I am wearing a helmet

↓

I am carrying a gun

↓

I work for Jabba the Hutt

↓

I am green-skinned

↓

2 My name is:

3 My name is:

4 My name is:

Find the **answers** on page 97.

Force Challenge
Test your knowledge of Chapter 2

Answer each question. If you need help, look back through the chapter.

Now that you have finished the second chapter of the book, take the Force Challenge to see what you know about the galaxy!

1. Find the sticker that best matches the description:

A droid with many arms used for maintenance and repair.

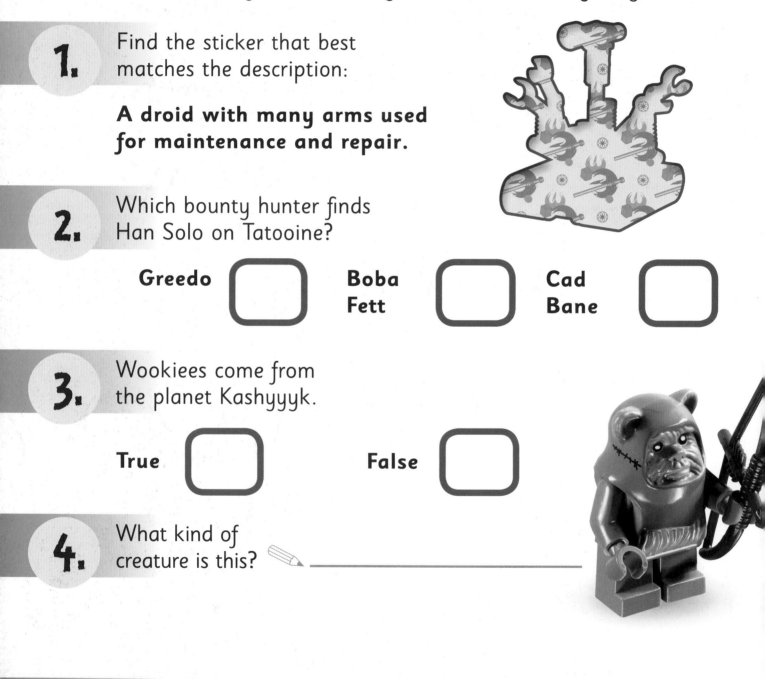

2. Which bounty hunter finds Han Solo on Tatooine?

Greedo ☐   **Boba Fett** ☐   **Cad Bane** ☐

3. Wookiees come from the planet Kashyyyk.

True ☐   **False** ☐

4. What kind of creature is this? ✎ _____

5. The Jedi Temple is on the planet ✎ _____

Find the **answers** on page 97.

Well done—you have finished the Force Challenge! Fill this scene with your extra stickers.

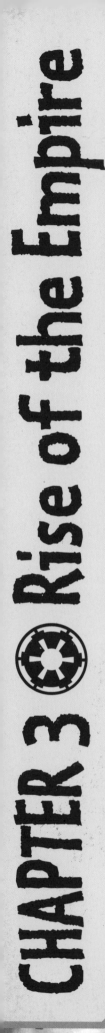

CHAPTER 3 ✦ Rise of the Empire

Darth Sidious

Emperor Palpatine is really Sith Lord Darth Sidious! Scheming and powerful, he wants to destroy the Jedi.

© 2016 LEGO

Darth Maul

Darth Maul was trained from a young age by Darth Sidious. He uses a double-bladed lightsaber and is a dangerous Sith assassin.

© 2016 LEGO

An evil Empire has taken over the galaxy. Emperor Palpatine uses an army of stormtroopers and secret Sith skills to get his own way. Many people do his evil bidding.

Count Dooku

Count Dooku was trained as a Jedi by Yoda until he turned to the dark side. For a while he was Darth Sidious's right-hand man.

Grand Moff Tarkin

Tarkin controls the building of Darth Sidious's superweapon, the Death Star. Sidious uses the superlaser to prove the Empire's strength in the galaxy.

Darth Vader

Darth Vader pledged service to his master, Darth Sidious, and vowed to destroy the rebels.

The Inquisitor

The Inquisitor is a mysterious figure hired by Darth Vader to hunt down Jedi. He dresses all in black and wears a helmet with a red visor to shield his face.

© 2016 LEGO

Evil Plans

Identify the evil villains

Using the dark side of the Force, these evil characters want to take over the galaxy and rule the Empire. They will fight anyone who stands in the way of their plans.

The galaxy will be ours!

Read the descriptions, add your stickers and identify each villain.

> After turning to the dark side, I want revenge on the Jedi. I will obey my Sith Master and hunt the rebels and the Jedi.

> I have turned my back on the ways of the Jedi. I will become the greatest dark side warrior ever.

© 2016 LEGO

© 2016 LEGO

1 I am ✏ _____

2 I am ✏ _____

Darth Maul
Trained from a young age by his Master Darth Sidious, Sith apprentice Darth Maul must battle Jedi Obi-Wan Kenobi and Qui-Gon Jinn when Sidious tells him to.

Darth Sidious
Darth Sidious is determined to rule the galaxy. He rises from senator to emperor in the galactic government and makes decisions that help his evil Sith plans.

Kylo Ren
Kylo trained as a Jedi with Luke Skywalker but then fell to the dark side. He admires Darth Vader and wants to be the most powerful dark side warrior ever.

Darth Vader
Darth Vader was turned to the dark side by Darth Sidious, who became his Sith Master. Injured in a duel with a Jedi, he now seeks to destroy Jedi and rebels.

I want to impress my Sith Master. I will use this mission to prove that I am worthy of being a Sith.

I will use my position of power to get my own way and control the galaxy. I want the Sith to be in charge.

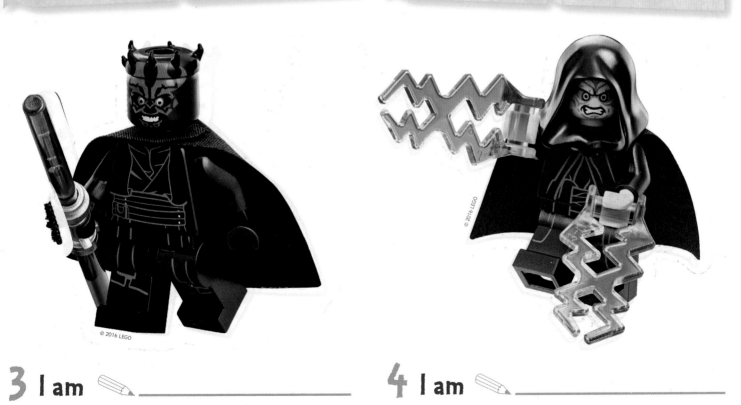

3 I am _____

4 I am _____

Find the **answers** on page 97.

Asteroid Escape

Help the rebels escape

A band of rebels are fighting to overthrow the Empire. Pursued by Imperial fighters, they navigate their ship, the *Millennium Falcon*, through an asteroid field to avoid the enemy.

Watch out for asteroids!

Add your stickers, then find a way through the asteroid field to escape the enemy.

Start

TIE Fighter

TIE fighters are versatile starfighters. Favored by the Empire, the roar of their engines is enough to scare anyone!

TIE Bomber

TIE bombers are used for attacking planets and targets in space with accuracy.

End

Millennium Falcon

The *Falcon* has been patched up many times. Despite the ship's shabby appearance, it is one of the fastest flyers in the galaxy.

Super Troopers
Color the soldiers' armor

The Empire uses many types of soldiers to rule the galaxy. As well as standard stormtroopers, they create lots of special units designed for different tasks and conditions.

Read about the troopers' armor, then color it in so they're ready for battle.

a brain so they can aim

Stormtrooper

Imperial stormtroopers are **fiercely loyal** soldiers of the Empire. Their **armor adapts** to different conditions and they attack in great numbers.

How would you **upgrade** the stormtroopers' armor?

Kashyyyk clone trooper

Serving in the Grand Army of the Republic, Kashyyyk clone troopers wear green and brown **camouflage** and a green visor.

Use different **shades** of green for camouflage.

Geonosis clone trooper

To match the dusty, rocky planet of Geonosis, these clone troopers wear **copper and brown armor** and helmets.

Design a new armor **pattern** for Geonosis.

Our blaster rifles are very powerful.

←wind, blowing sord

↑ extra amo

← arm blaster

Draw the **control panels** on the chest.

We are trained to fight in cold weather.

armor that will actualy protect him

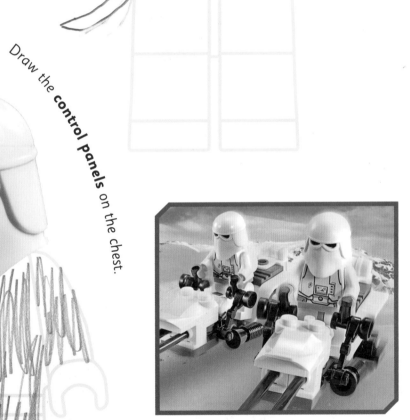

Snowtrooper

Equipped for extremely cold and **icy conditions**, snowtroopers wear insulated armor and a helmet with **built-in snow goggles**. Their armor has in-built heating units.

41

Starfighter Scramble

Complete the sticker jigsaw

Imperial and rebel starfighters battle against each other in the air. Starfighters are designed to be light and aerodynamic, and the pilots use their skill and bravery to outwit their enemies.

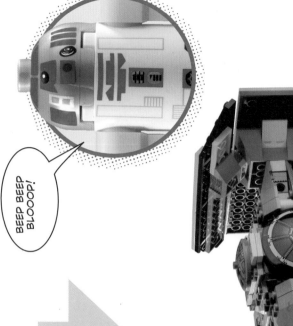

BEEP BEEP BLOOP!

Read about starfighters, then use the stickers to build Poe's X-wing

Vader's TIE Fighter

Darth Vader's TIE fighter is personalized for the Sith Lord. Curved wings, a deflector shield, and a hyperdrive mean Vader can compete with rebel X-Wings.

Jon Vander's Y-Wing

Jon Vander, known as "Dutch," joined the rebellion and flew a Y-Wing against the Empire during the Battle of Yavin.

Luke's X-Wing

When Luke joined the rebels, he started flying an X-Wing. He has flown in many battles.

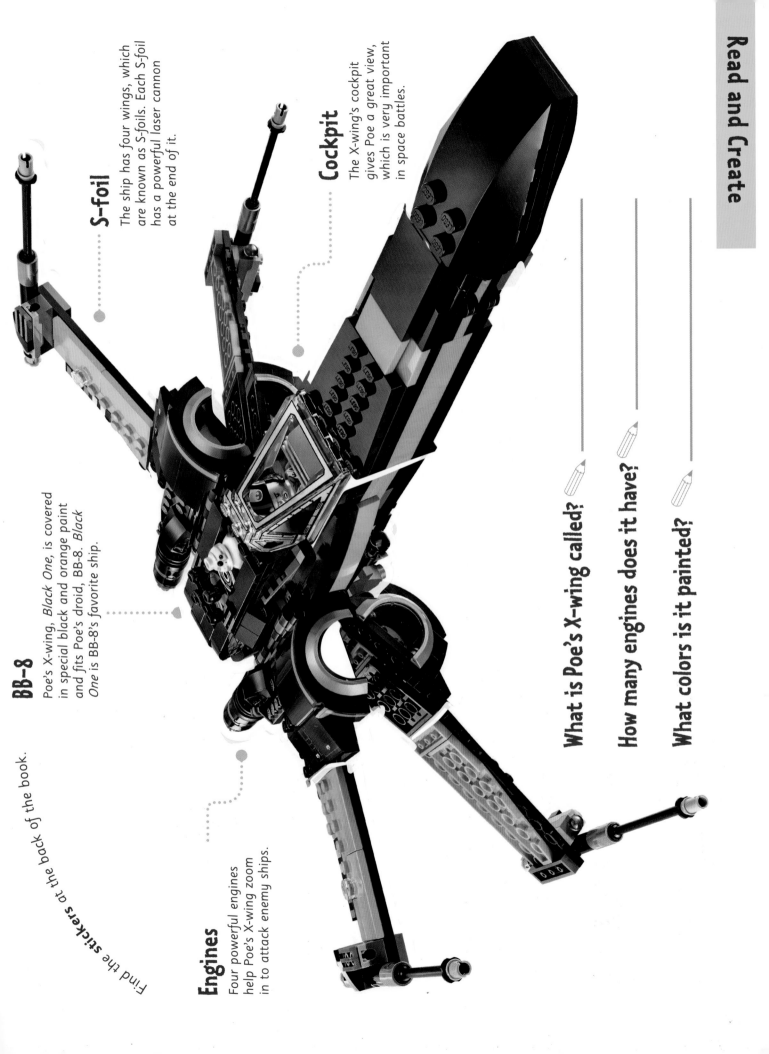

S-foil

The ship has four wings, which are known as S-foils. Each S-foil has a powerful laser cannon at the end of it.

Cockpit

The X-wing's cockpit gives Poe a great view, which is very important in space battles.

BB-8

Poe's X-wing, *Black One*, is covered in special black and orange paint and fits Poe's droid, BB-8. *Black One* is BB-8's favorite ship.

Engines

Four powerful engines help Poe's X-wing zoom in to attack enemy ships.

Find the **stickers** at the back of the book.

What is Poe's X-wing called?

How many engines does it have?

What colors is it painted?

Sith Apprentice
Design a new Sith apprentice

All Sith are members of the Order of the Sith. They follow the Rule of Two, which means that there can only ever be one Master and one apprentice at any one time.

Read all about the Sith, then draw a new apprentice for one of them.

Darth Sidious

Darth Sidious was once an apprentice of Darth Plagueis, a powerful Sith Lord obsessed with eternal life, before he became a Sith Lord himself.

Darth Vader

Since turning to the Dark Side, and after Count Dooku was defeated, Darth Vader has worked as Darth Sidious's apprentice.

Darth Maul

Darth Maul was trained as Darth Sidious's apprentice in a secret training facility on Mustafar but was defeated by Jedi Obi-Wan Kenobi.

Count Dooku

A former Jedi, Count Dooku took the Sith name of Darth Tyranus. He served as an apprentice to Darth Sidious after Darth Maul's defeat.

Draw a **weapon** for your evil Sith apprentice.

Will your apprentice wear a **colored cape** or **hood**?

This Sith is called: Bob

His or her Master is: No one

45

Armed and Ready

Draw the missing weapons

Work out which weapon belongs to which rebel and draw it in their hand.

Fighting back against the Empire's rule, a group of rebels on planet Lothal have come together. They use customized weapons as they try to free the galaxy— but their foes are well-armed, too!

Ezra

Ezra Bridger has a **unique** lightsaber that he built himself from materials that he found. It has a **blue blade** and a **blaster** in the handle.

Kanan

Kanan was in the middle of **Jedi training** when he was forced to go into hiding from the Empire. He never finished training, but he did build his own blue-bladed lightsaber.

Double-bladed lightsaber

This double-bladed lightsaber can be spun or thrown. This makes it very **dangerous** when used with **the Force**.

Blaster lightsaber

Built from scrap materials, this lightsaber is unique because it mixes a **traditional blade** with a **blaster pistol**.

Zeb

Zeb is the last of his kind from the planet **Lasan**, which was invaded by the Empire. He used to use his multifunctional weapon in his role as a **guard**—for defense, but also for attack.

The Grand Inquisitor

The Grand Inquisitor's job is to hunt down Jedi. His has knowledge of **the Force** and makes use of Force weapons for dark purposes.

Find the **answers** on page 97.

Jedi lightsaber

All Jedi must **build their own lightsaber** as part of their training. They are then personalized by their owner.

Bo-rifle

This bo-rifle is the weapon of the **Lasan Honor Guard** and is now very rare. It can be used to block attacks, but can also emit an electrical charge.

Force Challenge
Test your knowledge of Chapter 3

Answer each question. If you need help, look back through the chapter.

Now that you have finished the third chapter of the book, take the Force Challenge to show you're an expert on the Empire!

1. Find the sticker that best matches the description:

A starfighter that is unique to its Sith Lord pilot.

2. Which Sith Lord is also a respected senator of the galactic government?

Darth Sidious ☐   **Darth Vader** ☐   **Darth Maul** ☐

3. Snowtroopers are used on desert planets like Tatooine.

True ☐   **False** ☐

4. What kind of weapon is this? _____

5. The Inquisitor uses the Force to hunt down _____

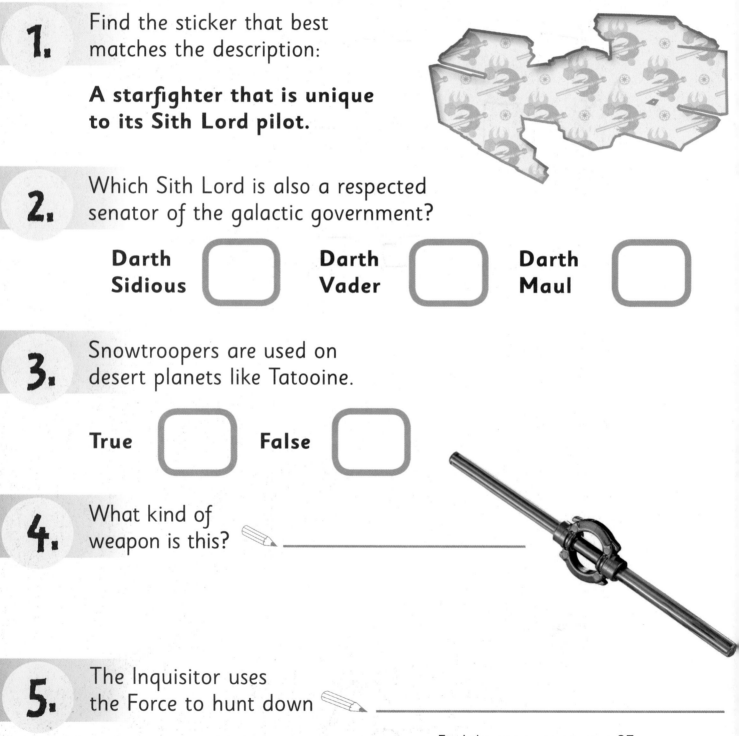

Find the **answers** on page 97.

Well done—you have finished the Force Challenge! Fill this scene with your extra stickers.

Luke Skywalker

Luke became a leader of the Rebel Alliance after helping to destroy the Death Star. He trained with Master Yoda.

Princess Leia

Leia is a key member of the Rebel Alliance. She stole the plans for the Death Star, so the rebels could destroy it.

Rebels are rising up from all over the galaxy to join the fight against the Empire. They are determined to remove Emperor Palpatine and restore peace.

Han Solo

The roguish ex-smuggler Han Solo is the pilot of the *Millennium Falcon*. He helps Luke destroy the Death Star.

R2-D2

Astromech droid R2-D2 plays a vital role in the rebellion when Leia entrusts him to deliver the Death Star plans to the rebels.

C-3PO

Loyal protocol droid C-3PO helps to rescue Princess Leia. He also fights on the front line with the rebels.

Lando Calrissian

Cool, confident Lando joins the rebels as part of the mission to find Han Solo after Han is captured by the Empire.

Chewbacca

Chewbacca joins the Rebel Alliance with Han Solo as the copilot of the *Millennium Falcon*.

Hoth Hideout

Find the lost weapons

The rebels have set up Echo Base on Hoth, but Darth Vader and his Imperial snowtroopers have found their hiding place. The rebels are forced to flee, leaving many weapons behind.

Read the descriptions and find the sticker to match.

How many lost weapons can you find? Write the numbers in the boxes.

Find the **answers** on page 97.

Rebel Luke

The rebels are surprised by the Imperial invasion. Lightsaber-wielding Luke and the rebels are forced to flee the planet.

Lightsaber

52

Rebel pilot

Rebel pilots try to hold back Imperial forces in their vehicles. They whiz around the AT-ATs, tying them up with tow cables and tripping them over.

Tow cable

Snowtrooper

Under orders from General Veers, snowtroopers enter Echo Base and chase out the rebels using blaster rifles.

Blaster rifle

General Veers

General Veers leads the attack to destroy the rebels' base. He uses a scanner to figure out where the rebels are hiding in the snow.

Scanner

TAKE THAT, SNOWTROOPERS!

Millennium Falcon

Complete the sticker jigsaw

The *Millennium Falcon* is one of the fastest ships in the galaxy. It has had many owners over the years, but the most famous are Han Solo and Chewbacca. They flew the *Millennium Falcon* during the rebellion against the Empire.

Cockpit

The spacious cockpit is on the side of the ship. The pilot and copilot sit beside each other.

Read about the *Millennium Falcon*, then use your stickers to complete it.

Missile Launcher

At the front of the Millennium Falcon is a powerful missile launcher. It fires proton torpedoes.

Gangsters

Han and Chewie have made a lot of enemies over the years. Now the nasty Kanjiklub gang has come looking for them!

Blaster

Han and Chewie upgraded the *Falcon*'s weapons. They added powerful blaster turrets to the top and bottom of the ship.

Reunited

Han and Chewie lost the *Falcon* after the Empire was defeated. Thirty years later they find it again, but now it has some stow-aways on board! Rey, Finn, and BB-8 used it to escape from the planet Jakku.

Engines

The *Millennium Falcon* has specially modified engines. These mean it can go much faster than most ships.

Armor

Han and Chewie are often getting into battles, so they added tough armor to the *Falcon*'s hull.

Secret Mission

Fill in the mission plan

The rebels have stolen important plans for the Empire's space station and weapon named the Death Star. Princess Leia must get the plans to the rebels. However, she is Darth Vader's prisoner, so she must act with great secrecy!

I must get a message to Obi-Wan!

Read the descriptions, then fill in the details of the secret plan.

Hidden message

Rebel leader Princess Leia has the plans for the Death Star. She has been captured by Darth Vader, so she hides the plans and a holographic message inside astromech droid R2-D2.

Tatooine landing

R2-D2 and another droid, C-3PO, land on sandy Tatooine. They are captured by Jawas and sold to Luke Skywalker's uncle. Luke hears Leia's message asking for help from Obi-Wan Kenobi.

Search for Obi-Wan

Luke takes R2-D2 to his friend Ben Kenobi who reveals himself to be Jedi Master Obi-Wan. They listen to Leia's message for help and Obi-Wan persuades Luke to come with him to rescue Leia.

Ship for hire

Luke and Obi-Wan hire smuggler Han Solo to help them to rescue Princess Leia. They disguise themselves as stormtroopers to fool the forces guarding her and free her from Darth Vader!

Read the story **opposite**, before you start.

THE REBELS' SECRET MISSION

1 Leia hides the plans for the Death Star in the astromech droid named ✎ _____ .

2 R2-D2 and C-3PO land on the desert planet ✎ _____ and are sold to Luke's uncle.

3 The message from Leia asks for help from ✎ _____ .

4 Luke and Obi-Wan hire ✎ _____ to help them.

5 They disguise themselves as ✎ _____ to rescue Princess Leia.

Find the **sticker** at the back of the book.

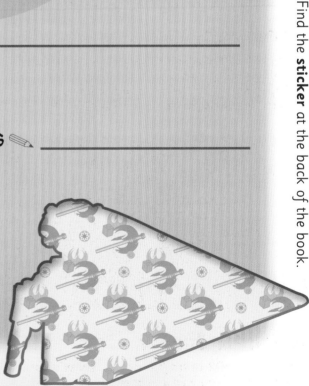

Find the **answers** on page 97.

Battle of Yavin

Fill in the speech bubbles

Using the stolen plans, the rebels organize an attack to destroy the Death Star. It is well protected and heavily armed so the mission will be extremely difficult and dangerous. Rebel pilots in X-wings begin the assault...

Read the comic strip and fill in the speech bubbles to complete it.

Luke leads the attack on the Death Star, with Darth Vader and TIE fighters in pursuit.

With help from Han Solo and the *Millennium Falcon*, Luke gets close to the Death Star's exhaust port. Using the Force, he fires his torpedoes.

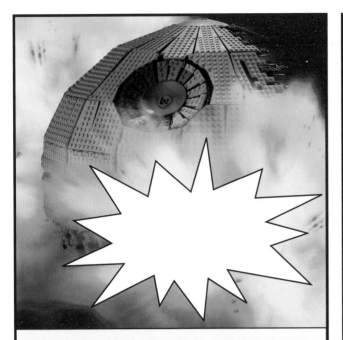

The torpedoes enter the exhaust port and explode, destroying the Death Star.

Luke quickly escapes the explosion. The rebels have won the battle!

Princess Leia awards Luke and Han medals for their bravery during the battle.

THE END!

Write a **diary entry** from Luke about the mission:

Daring Escape
Create a battle report

After learning that the Empire is building a second Death Star weapon, the rebels come up with a plan to destroy it before it can be completed. The Battle of Endor begins...

Read the story, then write and draw Han's battle report for the rebel leaders.

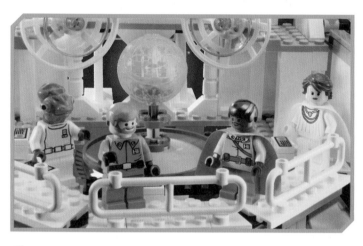

1 Rebel planning

The rebels are planning to shut down the shield generator that protects the Death Star. To do this, they must travel to the bunker contaiing the generator on the forest moon of Endor.

2 Scout-trooper chase

On the forest moon of Endor, the rebels, led by Han Solo, encounter scout troopers on speeder bikes and fight them off. Eventually, the rebels reach the shield generator.

3 Ewok attack

Outside the bunker, the rebels are surrounded by the Empire's forces. Ewoks arrive and launch a surprise attack on the stormtroopers, helping the rebels to fight back.

4 Destroy the bunker

The rebels enter the bunker and succeed in blowing it up. This shuts off the shield generator protecting the Death Star—leaving it more vulnerable to the rebels' planned starfighter attack. Watch out, Empire!

Decide what the most **important** parts of the story are and **write** about them.

Han's Battle Report
The Battle of Endor

_____

_____

_____

_____

_____

_____

A New Ride

Help rebel Sabine to decorate the rebel ship

Moving around the galaxy and fighting the Empire means the rebels need lots of vehicles. Sometimes they like to add a bit of color to their rides!

Read about the rebels and their rides, then decorate the spaceship.

Let's give this starfighter a new look to frighten the Empire!

Sabine Wren

Weapons expert Sabine likes to decorate everything around her—from her hair to her weapons and her vehicles! She loves bright colors, and is a force to be reckoned with.

Ezra's speeder bike

A stolen Imperial speeder bike, Ezra **customized** this with his favorite colors. It is built for **speed** and **firepower**.

The *Phantom*

This decorated **attack shuttle** is flown by rebel Ezra Bridger. It can dock inside its mothership, the *Ghost* and has a **detachable cockpit** for quick escapes!

You could add a **space background** behind the ship.

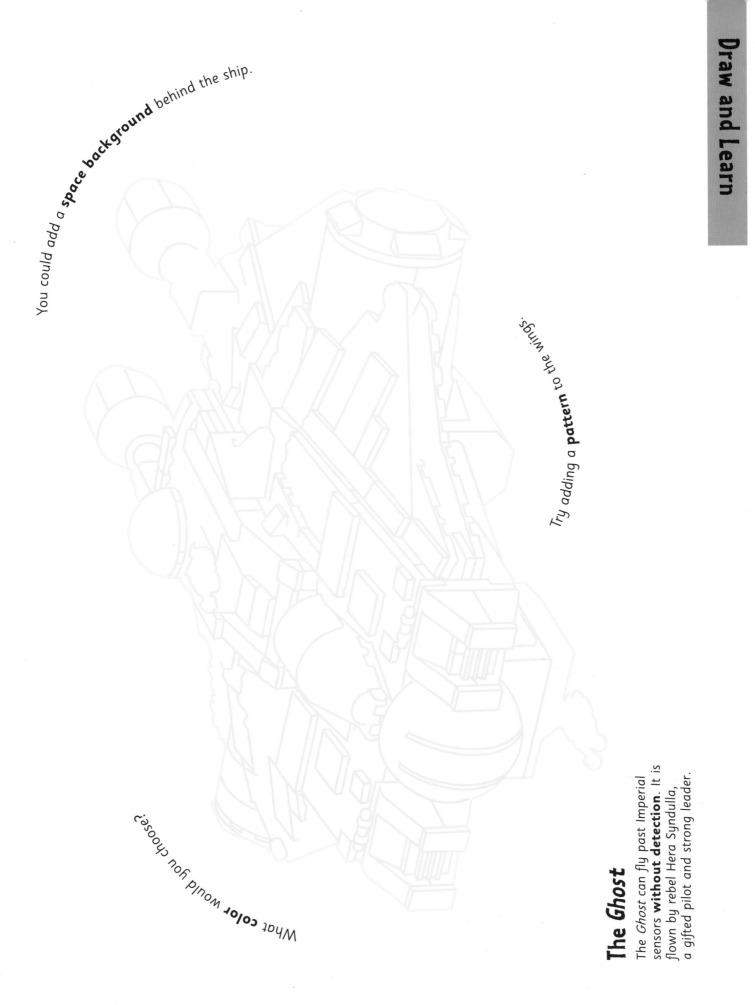

Try adding a **pattern** to the wings.

What **color** would you choose?

The *Ghost*

The *Ghost* can fly past Imperial sensors **without detection**. It is flown by rebel Hera Syndulla, a gifted pilot and strong leader.

Force Challenge
Test your knowledge of Chapter 4

Answer each question. If you need help, look back through the chapter.

Now that you have finished the last chapter of the book, take the Force Challenge to find out if you know how to defeat the Empire!

1. Find the sticker that best matches the description:

A very fast ship flown by Han Solo and Chewbacca.

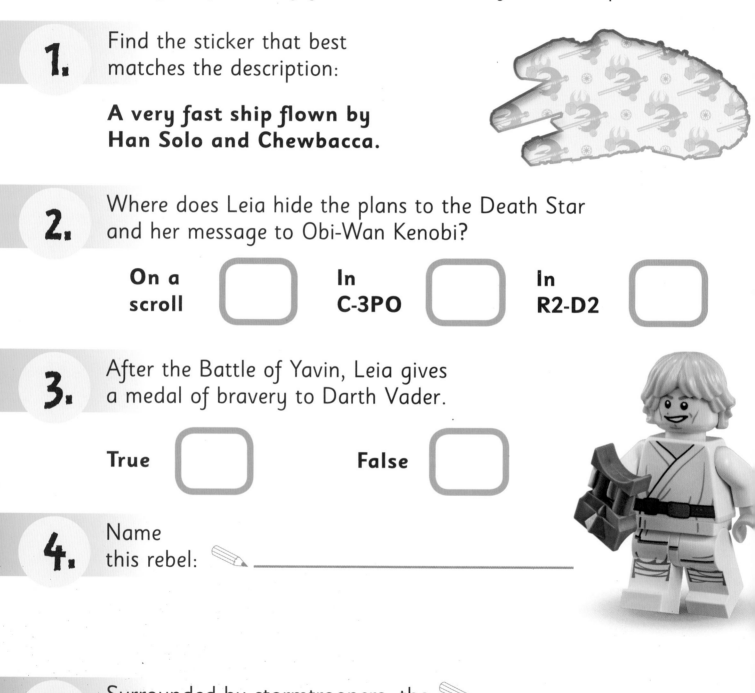

2. Where does Leia hide the plans to the Death Star and her message to Obi-Wan Kenobi?

On a scroll ☐   **In C-3PO** ☐   **In R2-D2** ☐

3. After the Battle of Yavin, Leia gives a medal of bravery to Darth Vader.

True ☐   **False** ☐

4. Name this rebel: ✏ _____

5. Surrounded by stormtroopers, the ✏ _____ help the rebels fight on the forest moon of Endor.

Find the **answers** on page 97.

Stickers for Chapter 1

Teaching

Mind tricks

Field trips

Duels

Knighthood

TIE Interceptor

Emperor Palpatine

Stickers for Chapter 1

Luke
Skywalker

Gunship

Jedi Luke

Force call

Anakin Skywalker

Obi-Wan Kenobi

Combat

Padawan
Ahsoka Tano

Star
Destroyer

Stickers for Chapter 1

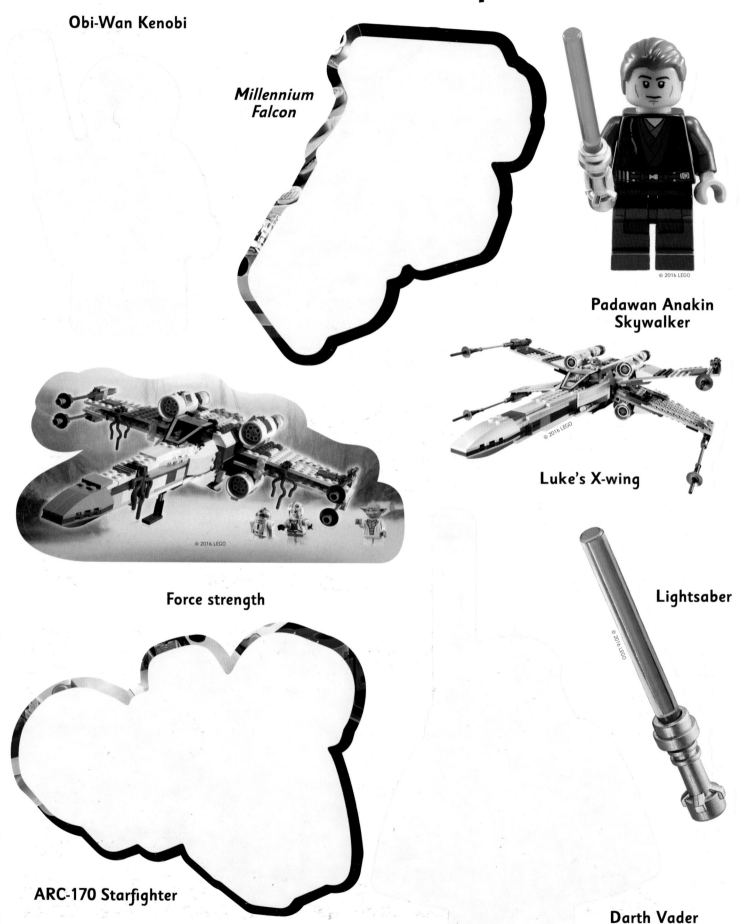

Obi-Wan Kenobi

Millennium Falcon

Padawan Anakin Skywalker

Luke's X-wing

Force strength

Lightsaber

ARC-170 Starfighter

Darth Vader

Stickers for Chapter 1

Yoda

Selection

Force movement

Extra stickers

© & TM 2016 Lucasfilm Ltd.

Stickers for Chapter 2

Jawas

Dengar

Droids

Gonk droid

Boba Fett

Tusken Raiders

Bossk

Gungan

R1-series droids

Treadwell droid

© 2016 LEGO

Stickers for Chapter 2

Cad Bane

Treadwell droid

Bounty Hunters

Astromech

Wookiees

C-3PO

R5-D4

Ewoks

Extra stickers

© & TM 2016 Lucasfilm Ltd.

Extra stickers

Extra stickers

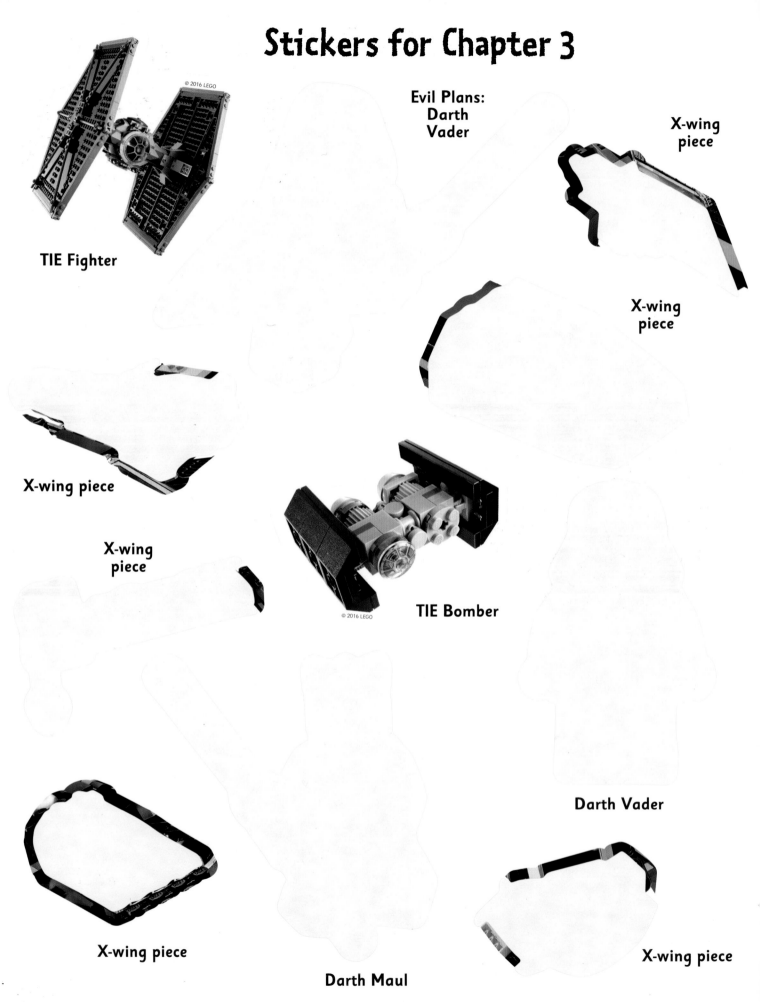

Stickers for Chapter 3

Evil Plans:
Darth
Vader

© 2016 LEGO

TIE Fighter

X-wing piece

X-wing piece

X-wing piece

X-wing piece

© 2016 LEGO

TIE Bomber

Darth Vader

X-wing piece

X-wing piece

Darth Maul

Stickers for Chapter 3

X-wing piece

X-wing piece

Evil Plans: Darth Maul

Darth Sidious

X-wing piece

Grand Moff Tarkin

The Inquisitor

Evil Plans: Kylo Ren

Stickers for Chapter 3

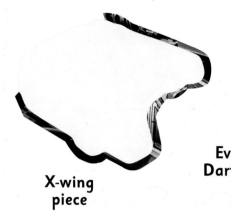

X-wing piece

Evil Plans: Darth Sidious

Vader's TIE-Fighter

X-wing piece

Count Dooku

X-wing piece

Extra Stickers

Extra Stickers

Stickers for Chapter 4

Princess Leia's message

Millennium Falcon piece

Millennium Falcon

General Veers

Millennium Falcon piece

Millennium Falcon piece

Princess Leia

Han Solo

Millennium Falcon piece

Rebel Luke

Stickers for Chapter 4

Luke Skywalker

Millennium Falcon piece

R2-D2

C-3PO

Millennium Falcon piece

Millennium Falcon piece

Snowtrooper

Millennium Falcon piece

Stickers for Chapter 4

Millennium Falcon piece

Millennium Falcon piece

Millennium Falcon piece

Chewbacca

Millennium Falcon piece

Lando Calrissian

Rebel Pilot

Extra Stickers

© & TM 2016 Lucasfilm Ltd.